Letters of

Love

& Legacy

A Mother's Tale of Her Journey to Her Son

By Marsha Flemmings

Table of Contents

Introduction

Since the age of 8, I knew I wanted to publish my writing and had set my goals on doing so by 21. At the time of writing this book I am 37 years old and for every year between 21 and 37 I have given myself every excuse not to achieve this goal. Actually, it's worse than I had considered. I really excused away 29 years. I criticized every word I ever wrote, convincing myself I didn't have the time or didn't know what to write about. I questioned what I had to share with the world that was so meaningful. I came up with every excuse/explanation/reason. Until……

At 35 years I had my first child and as many people say children do, Liam has changed me and my world in ways that I couldn't have imagined and only his presence could help prepare me for. Nearly all my life I heard that I seemed more mature than my age and I always *seemed* to be well rounded. I always *seemed* smart enough and a few years ahead of my age. The truth is I wasn't self-assured and confident for a long time. It only seemed that way.

My discovery process took a lot longer than I would have liked. I tried to figure me out for years. I wanted to feel accepted and connected to "great people". In my young mind these people would be anyone I perceived to be prettier than me, had more than I had or were better connected. I wasn't seeking to be popular. I just wanted to be accepted, to feel I was enough and to figure out where I fit in.

In my twenties I started to figure some of these things out, but many discoveries came through making mistakes or decisions that made me realize that isn't who I wanted to be. The biggest discoveries so far have come in my thirties and so for this very reason Liam's arrival in my life was God's perfect timing. I know who I am and while I'm still growing, the fundamentals of what I believe, who I am, how I treat people, how I want to be treated and appreciating myself are things that I have clarity on. Because of this clarity I am able to better guide him. God help the poor child if he had come into my life when I was 23, for example. I just didn't have this kind of strength of character. So what could I teach him about being his best self and how to treat others, or about success, commitment, love or faith?

True to my nature of overthinking, while I was pregnant I had a thought about what I wanted to ensure I would be able to leave with him once I am no longer here. Pretty morbid I know, but count on my brain to think of what to do in the worst case scenario. I just couldn't shake the thought of "how do I ensure he is able to keep and remember my words and the lessons I will share with him?"

I ultimately decided to write letters to him. Letters of Love to Liam I called them because every lesson was founded on the love I have for him and how that love drives me to do all I can to impact his future in the most positive way I know how. These letters were never meant to be shared with anyone but Liam.

In March 2018, a few months into the deepest self-discovery I had made to date, I had a thought while on a flight from the Bahamas to Miami and every fiber of my being told me that this was the direction I should head in. Suddenly, it made perfect sense that I would not have received one letter from his dad in this book. It wasn't because he didn't love him and didn't have his own thoughts that he wanted to share. It was because this was **my legacy** to him. I am certain this book will unfold so much more in my life than I can foresee because it was birthed from embarking on a journey to really become my best self and live my fullest life. This time there was more at stake and I couldn't excuse it away any longer because I now had this little human being to leave an example for and a legacy to.

It is my hope that any parent, grandparent, guardian, aunt, uncle, cousin, foster mother, adopted father...whomever that reads this book, is inspired to leave their own legacy and life lessons. You are invited to pour that legacy on to the pages of the free journal I am providing on my website www.marshaflemmings.com . I hope you are overflowing with the desire to share those things that truly matter to these young lives we have responsibility for.

Your message is your own, so think what's most important to you to share. What life experiences did you have that taught you some of your biggest lessons? What choices did you make that you would have done differently and why? Who is in the family that is no longer here that your child needs to know about (their contribution to the family and/or community)? What did you allow fear to keep you from? Or what family story is so hilarious and totally explains why everyone says Grandma is a total badass? What's your spiritual practice, if you have one and how has it helped you? What information do you have, that had your younger self known this, could have changed the course of your life? I am sharing with Liam these letters of love about, intention, finances, love, relationships, faith and more, not from a point of expertise but from what my own experiences have taught me. If one lesson from this book comes to his mind in a pivotal point in his life and he gives it any consideration, then this would have all been well worth it.

The truth is we can ensure that our words, our values, our influence, our guidance, our love and our legacy continue to speak for us to our loved ones long after we are gone. Even greater is that this influence will guide them to places where they make the difference to other lives and so your legacy continues.

What's your Legacy?

A Letter of Love to Liam

"The best love is the kind that awakens the soul; that makes us reach for more, that plants the fire in our hearts and brings peace to our minds." – The Notebook

Two weeks before I delivered my son into this world I sat down and wrote with contradicting feelings of fear and readiness. Here I was, about to welcome this new spirit whom I suddenly had the duty of guiding and helping to navigate his way through his own existence in this world. I thought, "Who in their right mind gave me that job?" Suddenly, an experience I had long desired seemed like a great deal of responsibility that I was now questioning if I had the tools for. After all, I am the one that went to the airport for an international flight without my passport a few short years ago. You can't get more unprepared than that.

I was sweating with thoughts of how would I know that I was making the right decisions in raising him or using the methods that would be most helpful to him. Amidst all of that, what I knew was that this little man whose face came to me in a dream almost 7 months before, I was ready to meet in person. I had more than enough discussions with him while he was cozily occupying the last space my bladder occupied over the last 8 months. I wanted to see him, to talk to him face to face. I wanted to protect him and get on about the business of watching him evolve.

To My Son Liam,

The choice to write to you is so that one day when I will no longer be here and you have decisions to make and are faced with the complexities life will throw at you, that somehow these words will help guide you or will somehow help make the decision that much clearer.

You were literally my Christmas gift. On December 25, 2015, your dad and I confirmed what we both believed. I was pregnant and our lives would soon change. I had bought the test nearly a week before and that morning I woke up and just had to know.

I had waited 35 years and you were my first baby I was blessed enough to hold, to look at, to smell, to love, to cherish and to help guide. I had waited, prayed and longed for you. You are the manifestation of my heart's desire & God's mercy towards me.

I already know you are a special child. Not only do I continually thank God for you, but I speak over your life daily. Know that you are a conqueror & your life has a definite purpose. I won't pretend to know your purpose; I am not your Creator. He knows and he will reveal it to you.

Your name, Liam, means "strong (willed) protector." Your middle name, Jru, means "God will add". Your dad and I chose these names for you with intention. We did not just consider what we wanted or liked. We thought about the characteristics that would be most useful in maneuvering this life and I personally thought of the characteristics I wish I would have displayed more consistently and with greater ease.

You were conceived in love. So much love. Is it too much for you that your dad and I knew the night you were conceived? I'm laughing as I can only imagine you don't want to know this, but I'm just trying to really help you understand just how much you were meant to be here. When I was two months pregnant I saw you in a dream sitting in a car seat just laughing. Your dad knew that we would be having a boy as well. I seriously think he wished you into existence. Finally your dad's aunt, who at the time I had not met and who didn't know I was pregnant, had a dream about a happy little baby boy playing at your dad's feet. One thing I knew for sure was my greatest gift and biggest blessing was on the way. Here I am today writing a book that will be my first published work because I was inspired by you. You have already changed my life in the most indescribable ways.

It's important that you know that I won't be trying to live your life for you, nor will your dad. We simply have the responsibility to love, guide and support you. You will have to walk your own path and trust that I am telling myself this too as much as I'm telling you. As hard as it will be for me not to hold on so tight that your wings can't spread, I know that my responsibility to you is greater than just shielding you from every possible danger. I understand my responsibility to be helping you learn how to identify dangers and avoid as many of them as you can and also to help you develop the skills that will equip you to handle the challenges and disappointments you will inevitably face. That much I am clear on and I will do what I have to.

Young Pa (we only call him that to facilitate his denial of his age) and G. Ma, my parents, are most excited to welcome their first grandson. Your GranGran and Grandpa, your dad's parents, are equally as excited to meet you. Your great grandmother has not stopped praying since she found out about you. I pray she never gets off her knees, along with all the other people that have lifted us in prayer. I can't begin to describe the love that awaits you from your family. You are already so blessed and I am so thankful.

You have a beautiful big sister bursting with excitement. She is only a few years older than you. She is your dad's first child. Do as your name says and protect her. You need her and she needs you. Every day she has asked when you are coming and I need you to love her as fiercely as she has anticipated you. Your uncle, despite how he tries to run my life, is my younger brother and most importantly my best friend. There is no one I count on the way I do him and while I know that we all build our relationships how we choose, trust me enough to know there is something very comforting in the wisdom of an older sister and the unfailing strength and support of a younger brother.

I have no idea what this world will look like in a few short decades and I can't fathom the challenges you may face wherever your journey takes you. No matter who you encounter or what the situation is, remember as Dr. Martin Luther King Jr. said, "Remember that darkness cannot drive out darkness, only light can do that. Hate cannot drive out hate, only love can do that."

Make no mistake, being the light and leading with love will not always be easy. It requires strength of character to consistently choose that path and it makes sense to me that you would be this man of great strength that I prayed for.

Never forget. You have it inside you to always choose that path.

Love Fiercely My Son.

What Is Your Intention

"Intention leads to behaviors which lead to habits which lead to personality development which leads to destiny." – Jack Kornfield

There were so many years that I had things I wanted to do and sincerely wanted to accomplish but I never decided and truly set them in my intention or became purposeful in achieving them. It amazes me because I took on projects that were not half as meaningful to me as the things I desired and I intended to make those projects a success and that's what I did despite all the obstacles.

I unconsciously thought, "hopefully one day" or "I don't know but I think I want to maybe try." Hence, fifteen years passed where I wanted to continue my education or travel to see more of the world among other things, but never got it done. I didn't make it my intention and work towards it. It was just a wish. This very first book never came to fruition until I approached completing it purposefully and intentionally. I completed a course with Cornell University while working a job that required on average 60 to 72 hours each week, took on a course to become a Certified Professional Coach, and started creating a business all while raising my son and participating in different groups and conferences to improve my speaking skills. Finally, I got sick and tired of wishing, waiting, hoping and praying that maybe someday. I had to own that someday wasn't going to magically happen. I had to move beyond wishing and decide this is what I am going to do and this is how I am going to do it. I also had to set some timelines and deadlines for myself, otherwise...nothing happened.

I had more on my plate than ever before, yet I thrived more swiftly than in the past. So what stopped me all this time? I hadn't decided! I hadn't made it a must. I wasn't intentional about making it happen. I gave myself a way out of doing it. In fact, I gave myself a million ways out. I decided the time wasn't there, I had nothing worth sharing, no one would be interested, I wasn't equipped or well connected. You name it, I said it!

The matter of intention goes even deeper because the truth is I set this book as my intention when my son became a part of my world and became the single most important reason for pushing myself to manifest all that I could, to not go down without giving it my best shot. After all I owe him my best. It's my responsibility to set him up to win and to show him that what you want to achieve requires discipline, consistency and the will to keep going. How could I encourage him towards his best self if I was not demonstrating that to him? I never kicked it into gear until I had a big enough reason, a "why" that was bigger than my life and for me that was Liam.

Dear Liam,

Living your life with intention is something so important that I hope you gain an appreciation for just how true this is in your early years. Life will always throw us curve balls, challenges, disappointments and so forth. The reality is that if we don't have a goal in mind or a target we are trying to hit, we will most certainly end up hitting targets we don't intend to, or worse yet, hitting nothing at all.

When you make a decision and set a goal in your intention it means you come up with a plan, a strategy, a series of steps to accomplish it. I found myself over the years telling my team, saying you want to buy a car or a house is not setting an intention. To become intentional about buying that car means you may:

☐ *Determine how much money you need to have and by when you want to have the car. So if you are giving yourself a year for example, you then divide the amount of money you need to come up with by 12 months or 52 weeks etc...you create a plan or strategy to get to the goal.*

☐ *Decide how much money you need, examine how you are currently spending, eliminate some unnecessary expenses and operate from the premise of saving as much as you can each week/month. You may also look for additional opportunities to make additional income.*

The alternative to this is staying with the desire in your mind with no active plan of action and possibly never being in a position to buy the car because you never made it your intention and approached it purposefully.

This is a big lesson for anyone with any desire because if we are blown in the wind and choose not to live intentionally then we are likely to live a life we don't want or is far less than what we could manifest.

Setting these action steps doesn't eliminate the fact that some days you won't feel like it. You may not feel like saving that money, or getting out of bed to go workout, but because you would have created a discipline or habit of doing so, it helps you continue to push forward even when you don't feel like it.

I told you in a previous letter the meaning of your name but let me remind you

Strong (willed) Protector/Guardian

Strong willed Warrior

Resolute Protector (Biblical Meaning)

Helmet of will (German Meaning)

While you were being born the song Stronger by Mary J. Blige was being played. Since I knew you were conceived I have prayed for your strength and spoke to you about your strength and I called them by name:

Emotional Strength

Spiritual Strength

Physical Strength

Mental Strength

Financial Strength

Strength of Character

While I prayed for other things for you, I focused on these purely from the belief that we all as human beings need this kind of strength to help us not buckle under the pressure of challenges that life experiences will surely present to us.

Now understand that I am fully aware that you will choose who you are and who you will become but because this is my intention, I will not only pray and speak to you, but I will consciously show you what strength looks like and place you in the presence of people who exhibit strength and as you grow engage in activities that help to build this in you. The point is that I am conscious of helping to build this quality in you and I am intentional in my efforts to make it happen. I have learned that zero effort will not give us our desires.

Do you know that for everyone we meet, aside from commenting on your features and how happy you are, the one thing that we always hear is how strong you are? This started in the delivery room with the doctors and nurses. It continued with your pediatrician when she learned that you were rolling over from your tummy to your back in your first month when many children do months later.

I do not believe there is any coincidence in all this. I watch you every single day and had I been a woman of lesser faith I would truly be daunted by the thought of raising you because the extent of your physical strength and strong will are very evident. I correct anyone that may use the word stubborn. I desire that you will grow up to be clear about what you want to accomplish, the strength to go after those things all with the wisdom to go after the things that are right. I prayed for your strength, how can I now call it something negative? I have also prayed for your wisdom, patience and a strong moral

17

compass. These will all help you and you will grow and learn when to lead with each quality.

So my son, live your life with good intentions. Know that the things you will go for, you are equipped and strong enough to endure what it takes to attain these things. You are gifted with the wisdom to learn the lessons along the way. Know that you have the strength to always love, give, help, reach, be , do, attain, overcome and most importantly you have the strength to ALWAYS do the right thing.

This journey is yours and I am right here with you supporting you the very best way I know how. Until recently, I did not always understand or practice being intentional. Now, especially because you have inspired me, every move, decision, investment, risk and step is with specific intentions. While I continue to grow in this principle, I know one primary intention I have for the rest of my life is to be the best version of myself so I can be the best mother I can be to you. You deserve it.

I love you Liam, always.

A Lesson in Faith

"Faith is the confidence that what we hope for will actually happen; it gives us assurance about things we cannot see." – NLT Bible

I was watching a movie called The Secret once and while I had some questions about what it was proposing and this universal law it was speaking about, there was particularly one statement I heard in it that made absolute sense to me.

One of the persons being interviewed likened faith to taking a journey in a car at night. The journey could be 200 miles. You can't see your destination when you first start out. In fact, at any given point in the night you can only see a few feet in front of you as the light from your car illuminates the road. However, if you travel that few feet, the light continues to project ahead of you unfolding the next few feet in front of you and so on and so on until the journey is complete.

Alarm bells went off in my head. I really needed to let this sink in. Innately, I hit panic mode the moment I can't figure something out and literally waste so much time doing that before I settle myself to work through a problem. I don't know if it's how I was raised, if it's my genetic makeup, or if it's because I was born a Scorpio with Jupiter in retrograde (not actually sure this is true). What I do know is that every experience in my life, anything I wanted to undertake but was afraid to because I didn't know how it was going to end, one of two things happened:

I stayed in place, never moved, never tried and never accomplished it

It resulted in a rewarding experience that I either achieved what I wanted, or more or at minimum learned so much that I could use to take me even further.

Dear Liam,

I hope to not confuse the common sense out of you because between this lesson in faith and explaining what love is, you may suspect your mother is crazy...but seriously, this is still an area I am growing in and learning to give up my need to be "in control". So for both of our benefit I will take this one in steps. Here we go.

What is faith?

It is that desire, that belief, that hope for something that has not happened yet, except in your mind and heart. That very belief itself is faith.

Why do we need faith?

Hmm. My first thought is for your sanity, but I'm really trying to be serious in my response and not scare you.

Maybe I should establish who you should have faith in. The most important in my mind is having faith in the source, the power and the being that created you. Let's think of some objects made by man:

A computer

An Aircraft

A Light Bulb

An Ironing Board

A Table

A Car

A Bathroom Hook

A Suitcase

An Umbrella

Whatever, it doesn't matter. The creation of each of these things had a very definite purpose. It was designed to do something specific. We may use them in other ways but the fact is they were created with a very specific intention and will best serve us when used the way it was designed to serve. Hence, the design of a thing is based on the circumstances around which it is expected to function. An ironing board won't have a car engine because the purpose for which it is built does not require that. The absence of that engine does not change or impact in anyway, the purpose the ironing board is meant to serve.

Should there be a problem with a car, in order to get it fixed it would make sense to take it to the creator of the car, or manufacturer in this case, to determine what's wrong and how to fix it. Even a mechanic has to learn about different types of cars because not all cars are designed the same, function the same etc. So the truth is the entity most informed and knowledgeable about this car is the person who created it. The manufacturer may not fix the car himself, but he will be able to say based on the problem you are having, here is how you can fix it. That's because he knows his design. He knows his creation.

We as human beings also have a source, a Creator that in His wisdom designed us equipped with what we need to function. Similarly, he knows what we need when things are off course and we are not functioning as we should in any capacity. So it is to our benefit to believe in his ability to correct what is going wrong in our lives, in his ability to provide what we need to produce the result He created us for.

Much like the inanimate objects I mentioned before, we as humans try to use things to "fix" or "heal" ourselves that are not meant for us and they will not work because the purpose for which we are designed does not require that and has no place in our lives.

So if you speak to a mechanic (I sure hope you will be at least remotely into cars since I insist on using them as examples), who explains how a car functions in simple terms, you will see that one thing is always sending a signal to the next or impacting the performance of the next. Meaning, if you push the start button, something is making contact with something else that creates the impact needed to start the car. Similarly if you press the gas pedal, the pedal is connected to something that is impacting something else and this entire relay of motion creates the movement of the vehicle or in the case of the brake it brings it to a stop.

We are the same as human beings. Not just in our body, but in living out our purpose. The people and things are placed in our sphere and we have different contact points that are meant to trigger us in some fashion. Everyone experiences these and becomes aware of them differently, but I think we share a common experience when we refer to a "gut feeling", an instinct etc. That's really just the inner workings our Creator designed us with to help keep us on track. This is why it is also important to stay true to that inner compass, because in so doing you will also develop faith in yourself. The relationship you have with yourself is as important as any other, if not moreso.

I have many stories to share with you and you won't be able to escape them, your grandparents used to kill your uncle and I with old sayings. So I will return the favor. One of the most recent experiences I had was back in November 2017. For days I had been so pensive about my next step, what I thought it should be and just believing that I needed some guidance or someone to bounce ideas off of. Now there was no shortage of people in my life to talk with, but I just was so insistent that the person must have had this kind of experience, this kind of success in this particular area blah blah blah.

One morning as I prepared for work, a particular lady came to mind. I quickly dismissed her from my thoughts because she wasn't someone I knew very well. We knew each other through work and four months prior, we connected because she is a lover of babies and wanted to meet you. In my mind she may have been a good person to speak with, but I just saw her as super successful, poised, well put together and just seeming to be busy living the life of her dreams that I was intimidated to ask for her time. In the instant she came to mind I dismissed her and thought that if I come up with no-one else to ask then maybe I will try to reach out to her.

There in my bathroom, I heard a voice I had heard a few times already in my life. I believe this to be the voice of God (and I say this knowing that I risk people looking at me like, "who in the name of over 2 billion people on the planet are you?") . But...this was my experience. I heard as clear as day in a matter of fact tone: "That's not what you need to reach out to her and ask. You need to ask her what it is I have told her to do that she hasn't done. You need to let her know it is possible, there is time and all she needs she already has or will be provided for her."

I immediately dismissed that thought. I was not about to reach out to this woman who I saw flying in private jets, speaking to crowds of people on different stages and living her best life and say anything but congratulations, how did you accomplish that and can you show me a thing or two. Even in my own mind I couldn't fathom this woman had anything she wanted to do that she hadn't done. She was accomplished, very accomplished, she was impacting others and SHE had a beautiful family. What else was there? I proceeded to carry on about my business.

As I was about to leave home that morning I was reminded that I had been given an assignment. I was not thrilled. This had literally already happened to me six times in my life that I could remember. Each time I realised why it was important to be obedient. For that reason alone I turned back, placed my bag down on the dining room chair and took my phone out. I took several deep breaths and uttered a prayer (if I could call it that). I had the audacity to tell God that I'm trusting Him to not make me look stupid in front of this woman. The nerve I had!

I recorded a voice message and I can't recall for sure, but I wouldn't be surprised if I started over a few times. I wasn't at all in my comfort zone. However, I ultimately sent a message, put my phone away and said, "I did it and I'm done." I exited my home either muttering to myself or complaining in my mind, "God I hope you are happy because if this woman thinks I'm crazy or wonders what in God's name I'm talking about it's going to be a problem."

I had to pick up a friend of mine, so by the time I got to work about 15 minutes had passed. We were walking in and I felt my phone vibrate. I checked my messages and I opened a video message with this beautiful, sophisticated woman, sitting in her car in tears talking to me, voice cracking and just sobbing. I quickly closed the message and turned to my friend in disbelief. I hadn't listened to more than about 3 seconds of the message. I was trying to continue walking and avoid telling my friend what was happening, but I was next to tears myself. Then my phone rang and it was her calling. I remember fighting tears and asking God, "what is this?".

I did not know what to do with myself. I had nothing else to say to her. I told her all I heard. What else could I say? I answered and couldn't even get through saying good morning as she was bawling on the phone. She tried to speak and she couldn't. Being the ball of emotions I am, tears flowed from my eyes. When she could, she went on to share with me all she would have shared in the video I had not yet watched but with more details.. She opened up to me exactly what the message was about and how just the day before she called her mother

25

broken about the fact that she knew this was something she was supposed to be doing but felt it wasn't possible with all the things she is already doing. She didn't see how she could possibly make time and she didn't know where to start or what she would need to get going. I felt tension in my chest from the realization that the specific things I spoke to answered those very thoughts.

She was mindful to repeat, as she had done in the video, that I had been used to speak directly to her, that she was glad I was obedient to the voice of God and that the three specific points I gave to her were exactly the things she had been complaining about to her mother. The most important thing that we both walked away certain of, was that this whole experience was not about either of us. Our Creator had a job He needed to get done. He wants to use her to get it done and in that moment He needed to send her that message and for whatever reason he chose me to deliver the message.

It took true belief in what I couldn't see to be obedient and follow the instructions I was given. I want to be practical with you while speaking about these things because I know how it feels to want some "real life" guidance and advice and be met with what sounds like "spiritual rantings". However, I also have to be true to my experiences and beliefs and I know that no one can know more than the source that created them. Obviously, the Creator in any scenario has more intelligence and power than the thing it has created.

2012 was a particularly trying year that was only going to lead to an even more trying 2013. I had not met your father yet and at that time I was in the middle of a relationship I knew was not for me. What's worse I knew this for well over a year, shortly after I would have started that relationship and I have no excuse for why I hadn't made my way out. However, I realize now, that this mess I would have created for myself held some of my most profound lessons and personal challenges. The process of refining gold is a harsh one. Put through fire and harsh chemicals, gold emerges pure and separated from any impurities. So too, we endure challenges for the purpose of refining us. I was in the midst of that.

November 2, 2012 a few hours after my birthday would have ended, that relationship ended when for the first time in that relationship and in my life, I experienced a man I was in a relationship with becoming physically aggressive and displaying threatening behavior. So much so that in the early hours of the morning I ran from my home in fear of what he may be tempted to do. I remained away from my home for a few days as he refused to remove his belongings and return my vehicle. Yes, I could have called the police, but I was living on a small island and wanted to preserve my privacy as best as I could. I wasn't trying to bring attention to my experience. I simply wanted it to end. Eventually it did, but not without a series of events unfolding like I was watching the latest suspense thriller on TV.

Much to my surprise, I found out on November 11, 2012 that I was pregnant. It's odd to consider I am sure, but I couldn't fathom how and when it would have happened as things were strained between us for a long time. I was beside myself. Here I was, finally out of this relationship, relieved it was behind me and now I was pregnant? Surely God was playing a cruel trick on me. I will tell you honestly my son, I grappled with this. I thought of how I could possibly live knowing that not only was I now permanently tied to this man, but that I would have to be in consistent dialogue and contact with him when I had just experienced what I thought to be the worst of him. I don't hate him and I don't sincerely believe him to be an evil person. I saw him as someone that in an effort to hold on to something that was slipping away from him, lost control. I just wasn't comfortable in his presence after what had happened. I was lost.

My truth is that I considered not moving forward with the pregnancy. I can't describe to you the pain and fear in my spirit because I was disappointed in me that I allowed myself to be in this place. I took a trip to see the family in Miami and to clear my head because in the cloud of all that had happened I couldn't think clearly. I remember going to sleep that Thursday night and waking up that Friday morning with your Uncle looking at me. My first words to him were that I made a decision and I'm keeping the baby. While we did have a discussion his first words were ok, so let's start planning. I was afraid because I had no idea what I was in for, but I felt something that I need you to pay attention to. There was a kind of peace or calm that I felt in the space at the top of my stomach, in the opening of my ribs. I need you to connect with that feeling. It is your compass, your GPS to help keep you on track when you are heading in the right direction. Ultimately, I knew that living with the alternative was a weight I couldn't take on.

Several weeks later, I made it known to him that I was pregnant and that while we were not going to be together we had to figure out how to co-parent. He didn't seem surprised by the news. He was calm but pleased and I remember thinking that was odd. I had a few weeks of terrible morning sickness, only this was "All Living Day Sickness." To his credit, he was very attentive and supportive. I had settled into the fact that I was about to be a mother and that this was going to be my life and though it wasn't the design I hoped for when I envisioned a family, this was the reality of it.

We took an unplanned visit to the doctor so he could hear the heartbeat, as I had previously done all that on my own. Laying there on the examination table, with him next to me intently watching the screen and waiting for the first sounds, I became concerned that I didn't hear the heartbeat immediately. After a few seconds and a telling look on the face of the ultrasound technician, I asked if I shouldn't be hearing the heartbeat and he responded, "allow me a minute." I looked at the image on the screen and as small as that fetus was a part of me knew something was wrong. I started to panic as the technician acknowledged that he was not detecting a heartbeat, questioned if I had any pain or bleeding and asked to be excused to call the doctor. I immediately picked up my phone and did a google search for no heartbeat and before I could finish I saw a drop down list of no heartbeat at 12 weeks, 10 weeks, 8 weeks etc.

I clicked on 11 weeks. I saw so many stories of women who had previously heard the heartbeat of their unborn child and under varied circumstances found themselves at the doctor's office or hospital without a heartbeat. I found only one story where a woman shared her experience and stated that she told the doctor that she was not having a procedure done and if her body was in fact rejecting this baby that it would have to do so without any help from her. She ended by saying that the day she was writing that her son was already passed his second birthday. With that search I was more panicked than before. My voice started to crack as I spoke.

29

Finally, the Head Doctor at the lab walked in, explained what the technician reported and said that she called my doctor who made a U-turn from heading to the airport for his Christmas vacation in Trinidad. After what felt like hours later, he walked in. I fell apart. He told me the same thing and said he was going to conduct the ultrasound himself. He did. There was no heartbeat. I told him to check again. No heartbeat. Upon my next request, he laid his hand on mine and said, "Marsha, I would never do this to you if I wasn't sure." He said your baby is gone and in fact doesn't show any signs of development past 8 weeks. He said, "I cannot let you leave here, take the plane back to that small island knowing you won't have medical care. I won't chance it. We have to do this procedure and the only thing you need to tell me is what hospital you want to go to because I am taking you both there now."

So much of what followed seemed like a dream to me. I called your grandma. My hands were shaking as I tried to dial and once she answered I realized there were no words coming from my mouth. I was truly overcome with the deepest grief I had ever felt. I don't know how to describe it other than a heaviness that somehow left a hollowing in my stomach. My throat and chest felt like I had swallowed a plum whole. So much happened and then I moved from pain to fear as realised I was going to be put under when the anesthesiologist was introduced to me. I was given papers to sign. They were explained to me, but my mind couldn't keep up with processing all that was happening. And so I signed, wondering if I had just signed my life away.

My mind shot to the movie with someone who received general anesthesia and felt every cut but couldn't move or speak. The experience is called Anesthesia Awareness. I had enough clarity to ask if my vitals would be monitored and oddly asked about what if I had a clot. The doctor explained all the precautions he was taking to ensure my safety.

I was rolled into the operating room and just like that I was staring at my own movie, laying on the operating bed with these huge flood lights shining down on me. The anesthesiologist approached me, told me he would apply the anesthesia now and that I should count backwards from 20. I remember getting to somewhere about 9 and just as I thought to have the biggest meltdown the world has ever seen because the anesthesia wasn't working, I felt my body tingle and that was it.

The days and months that followed were painful. My heart hurt the most. It's so amazing looking back how I was so perturbed by discovering I was pregnant only to feel complete devastation of the loss of this child that I had started to look forward to. How could this be? How is it that I chose to do what was right, what my heart could live with, what my faith led me to but this was the outcome? It didn't make sense to me.

The months that followed were even more trying. He had become someone I didn't know, that is if I ever did know him. I tried to live at peace with him, but like a man on fire trying to save himself, he was destined to harm even the very people who would try to help him. I own my naivety, though your uncle warned me that when a relationship ends two people can possibly be friends but it can't happen right away. I guess I must have thought that he was sharing the loss with me and foolishly thought that only he understood.

For the next year and a half, he would terrorize my life. We were not in a relationship and not involved. He was just simply someone I shared a portion of my life with that I didn't have the good judgment to create the distance between us after all that had happened. This resulted in him calling and talking to anyone who he felt would listen in an attempt to undermine me, all while trying to encourage me to try and salvage the relationship. He would let the air out of my tires and on two occasions escalated his aggression enough to grab me by my clothes so forcefully they ripped.

The matter only got worse when he learned that I was dating your father. For almost two years, I lived in utter darkness. Not just the darkness of his actions, but my mind had become engulfed. I had endured enough and was sick of it all. I couldn't wrap my head around why things took such an ugly turn. Don't get me wrong my love, I had made my share of mistakes in this entire thing. I stayed in a relationship long after I discovered it wasn't right for me, not because I thought he was a bad person, but it just wasn't for me. I stayed and didn't try, didn't work at it, didn't care, threw myself in work and just didn't exhibit what a thoughtful person should.

It took me a long while, but I had started some time before that distracting myself with running. Your Auntie Karen and I would discuss the books we were reading and I realized afterwards that all these things were positioned in my life to help get me through. I had met and worked with Karen 3 years before and only in the last few months had we forged a true connection. The conversations we had many times were the speck of light in the darkness that had consumed my mind during that time.

In the end, one day as I was in the process of gradually finding Marsha again, I thought about why it all had happened the way it did and what I would have done differently. There in the privacy of my home, I heard the answer that gave me the kind of peace that only the truth can. This was all a test of my faith. I do not believe that child was ever meant to be. I believe wholeheartedly that child was never destined to be born. I had walked myself into a situation I had no business in which resulted in some of the darkest days where I contemplated some of the worst things that I am not proud of. However, through it all, my Creator was patiently waiting to see if I would trust Him enough to know that He would guide me through.

A lack of faith can cause you to become so broken and lost in trying times. A lack of faith can cause you to stay in one place, never moving and never starting the journey. So the choice is yours. You can either risk staying in the same place and become, experience and do nothing. Or you can exercise faith move forward and take from the experience what you need to get to become better.

The choice is yours my son.

Rooted in Relationships

"It's not what we have in life, but who we have in our life that matters" – Unknown

Let me first clarify that family, in my opinion, is not simply persons connected to us by blood, marriage or adoption. Our foundation is in the very relationships we start to cultivate from the very beginning, how we impact those relationships and how they impact us, be they related by blood or not. Family is more about the people, who through it all are willing to stick it out with you, they support you and you support them; that through disagreements and serious misunderstandings no one gives up on the other. Family is about the people that protect you fiercely, but are also are not afraid to hold a mirror up to you to see yourself.

The reason this is foundation is because it is through these very relationships and experiences that we start to shape and define who we are. We discover what we believe, what we don't believe, what we like and dislike, how we want to be treated and learn how to treat others. Have you ever been able to look at your actions in any situation and identify traits of your family in your response or mannerism, especially of parents or guardians? In some cases, when we see a quality that is less than admirable in someone close to us, we decide that is **not** what we want to be. So even if we come from a "dysfunctional" family, it is all still shaping and influencing us in some way.

In a world of broken homes, shattered families and homeless children, it's important that while we recognize and acknowledge the sense of stability, comfort and belonging a family can bring, it's more important that we are examining all our relationships, how they function, how they serve us and how we serve them.

Dear Liam,

Your maternal grandmother was one of five children for your great grandmother and the only girl. For a host of reasons she was raised by a couple that were not her biological parents. One conversation with her about it and the feelings of wonder and gratitude are palpable. While she ultimately grew to know her siblings and her biological parents, it is understandable that a part of her wonders why that decision was made. However, there is also a huge part of her that remains forever grateful for the lovely couple who did raise her. Her belief is that they provided for her what her parents may not have been able to and attributes much of her success to the principles they instilled in her as a child.

While they took great care of her, they also raised their niece and over the years opened their hearts and home to many other children that were not their own. She spoke often, while I was growing up, about the heart they had, how they loved her, how they provided for her and treated her as if she was their own. What was unknown to them was the resentment harbored by not only their niece, but also other members of their family. Your grandmother, however felt it in every little comment that was made to remind her that she was not "family".

As the years passed and they endured the loss of the only father your grandmother grew up knowing, Papa, as she called him, the challenges with the extended family grew. As talks surfaced about what your grandmother could possibly stand to inherit should Mama pass away, so did talks from some of the family surface about plans to ensure G. Ma got nothing even if it meant taking her life.

Once she got wind of this, it took her no hesitation to decide it wasn't worth it to her. She had never learned from her parents that property or possessions were what mattered. In fact she learned the very opposite. Watching their generosity to many and living her own experience with them, taught her to help others, feed those who are hungry, support those who may be having challenges in their lives and always extend a helping hand. They taught her to give. So it wasn't in her nature to simply take or be overly concerned with acquisitions when the example she saw for years was about giving freely.

She ultimately decided to move away for the sake of her life and in the hopes of making it clear that all she was interested in was the ability to say thank you and give back to Mama, who had so freely given to her.

So here she was, a young woman, removed from her biological family, welcomed and loved by strangers but having to abandon their home as their family grew seemingly jealous or insecure. She was finally now out in the world without a sense of family.

I remember growing up and always hearing her sing this song, "I'm nobody's child. I'm nobody's child. Just like a flower I'm growing wild". I always sensed that it came from an emotional place but was still a bit too young to fully appreciate the place in her being that song came from.

When she started a family of her own, she was adamant that no one would be raising her children for her. Wherever she went, there your uncle and I would be. So much so that she would never travel without us if she was leaving the country. She was determined that no matter how little or how much she had, no matter what turn life may take, her children would remain with her. As irony would have it, the first time she decided to chance leaving the country and not taking us, is the same year I broke my arm and Uncle Lance suffered from a skin condition that had water bumps breakout all over his body, then leaving dark marks where they were. Needless to say she never did that again.

The relationship I had with her, particularly in my teenage years, was rough. Her relationship with Uncle Lance also has had its rough patches. What happened is G. Ma. held on super tight. She was very restricting and didn't entertain the thought of us going anywhere without her supervision. I mean, I was a member of a church in our community that was a six minute walk away from our home and even as a teenager, to attend some events or services in the evenings, a group of church elders had to come to the home to collect me from her and the same group would escort me back home. I remember back then being embarrassed that this was the case. However, the older I grew and the more I understood her own experience and how she interpreted it, the more I understood what motivated or influenced her behavior. Back then I thought she was just crazy and the toughest mother on planet earth. Only through time, maturity and some good discussions with her did I, over the years, gather that she was simply a woman who in her childhood struggled with feelings of abandonment and wanted to protect her children so fiercely that they would never have to question if she loved them and wanted to protect them. Now would I use her methods? Maybe not. Do I understand what was driving her? Yes. Do I think she was doing the best she knew how or what she thought was right? Absolutely. Have I used this as a learning experience? Well for your sake I sure hope I have.

I could provide you with so many examples to reinforce that there will be a lot in life that will shape who you are and who you become. However, none so powerful as the relationships we form and what they teach us. I challenge you to learn from each relationship. I challenge you to find the lesson and the blessing in even the most challenging relationships or challenging situations within our relationships. It is not so much what happens in these relationships as it is how you think, feel and respond to what happens. There is always something to take away from every interaction that can serve you and help you in some way.

Benefit from each connection,

Love You My Son.

Love is...

"Love is an action. Never simply a feeling." – Bell Hooks

So many people when you ask them to tell you what love is stumble through an explanation. I have been one of those people! Love certainly feels like a complex thing, but I have found that it is more simple than complex. The complexities are introduced when we confuse other emotions with love or allow other emotions to overpower our expression of love. More importantly, I believe that until we have experienced self-love, it will be hard to cultivate and preserve loving relationships with others.

Self-love is not arrogance or conceit. It is consistent behaviors towards you that are aimed at speaking to and calling the best version of yourself forward. This is displayed in the decisions that you make for yourself, how you treat yourself when you make a mistake, how you recognize your efforts when you achieve a goal. How do you care for you?

For some, self-love can take time to understand and practice. Expressing love is a practice and it takes discipline. I can only explain this as simply as I have experienced it and have learned to express it. Have you ever had a loved one who was ill? Let's say a diabetic who shouldn't be eating certain kinds of food and they wanted to have something you were having. You insisted they couldn't have it, but you felt bad for depriving them of it. Ultimately, you knew it would be in their best interest. Overriding that immediate feeling of wanting them to get the gratification and sticking to what's in their best interest takes discipline. Now don't get me wrong, there can be many variations to the circumstances that may allow people to say love can be expressed in other ways, but what I'm trying to explain is that love isn't necessarily the most obvious or gratifying option in that moment. I believe love guides your actions to be in accordance with what is the greater good for the recipient of your love.

MY LOVE ☺,

I'm going to do my best to explain how I understand love. For me, the bible describes it perfectly. It explains that love is kind and patient. While it does start off by saying what love is, it also quickly tells us what it is not. It gives us a way to evaluate behaviors and how we treat each other. That way, we know when we see pride, arrogance, selfishness, greed, impatience, dishonoring others or envy that these behaviors do not reflect love. This is true in regards to how you treat yourself, how you treat others and how they treat you.

Sometimes you may find yourself thinking or behaving in the very ways that love isn't. When you do, it's your responsibility to pause, control your thoughts, emotions and actions. Recognise that you have the ability to decide to show more kindness, patience, tolerance and generosity. You won't be perfect honey, but you are strong enough to identify your unloving behaviors and to become better. You may have the good fortune of having trusted friends who will be honest with you and hold that mirror up for you to be able to see yourself, but also know you already have the wisdom and the strength to listen to your internal moral compass.

Love is long suffering and love endures. What that means, to me, is sometimes you may find that you love someone and something may be wrong. They could be sick, going through a tough time that nothing you do helps, or you could be having a huge disagreement with them. Displaying love is not always easy or comfortable. Sometimes it means that you will choose to endure through the sickness, the misunderstandings and the hurt. You work your way through the challenge when love exists. This is the very reason I told you it requires strength. It isn't always easy and it isn't always the fairytale experience you see on TV. Even in transitional stages of relationships, love still reinforces these behaviors. So a romantic relationship, for example, can come to an end without either person dishonoring each other, being unkind, quick to anger or revengeful. It is possible because we can choose love, which means we can choose how we respond.

Your uncle and I were having a conversation one day, years before you were even born. At this time, your grandparents would have been together over 30 years. He happened to be home with them, but in a separate room. He described hearing G. Ma in one of those belly shaking, eyes tearing, can't breathe laughter for a long while. So much so that he was intrigued enough to find out what the conversation was about. It's not that your grandmother never laughs, but to hear her laugh like that with your grandfather was not an everyday occurrence.

Your grandparents are polar opposites in almost every sense. Your grandfather naturally loves to have a good time, be the life of the party, dance at the first beat of music no matter where he is, go on adventures, is friends with nearly everyone and "just live" as he says. Your grandmother is much more reserved with a small handful of friendships, most of which have spanned more years than her marriage. She leads with generosity, is level headed and has an aversion to adventure. So naturally, as you can imagine, for years I wondered about their compatibility. I suppose your Uncle may have too.

I remember him saying that maybe he and I were looking at relationships all wrong because through all the ups and downs, here they were decades later, sharing the heartiest of laughs with her simply telling your uncle, "your dad cracks me up."

It may seem like such a simple thing, but I understood where he was coming from when he said so many of us believe that relationships, and specifically love in romantic relationships, look a particular way. We usually think that interests have to be the same, the approach to handling life, finances, heartbreak, loss and wins have to be the same for a relationship to make sense. Specifically, I remember him speaking about the feeling of happiness and many people making an assumption that in the context of a relationship, if you don't experience that every day that the relationship is doomed or is failing. The fact that you are responsible for your own happiness is another matter. Please remember that in relationships it's not for another person to make you happy, but they can add to your happiness for sure.

My parents were two very different young people from different places in rural Jamaica, who found each other as a young police officer and a young teacher, who came from different backgrounds, started a family and provided for their young family through lots of hard work and sacrifice. They did this while maneuvering the challenges that arose from their different approaches to life, the challenges they faced individually and the general challenges that arose during the course of the relationship. Here they were on that day proving that two people could still find comfort and laughter in each other even after over 30 years of ups and downs. My brother got me thinking that maybe I did have it wrong.

So what makes two people so different, who would have experienced the bumps and rough patches in their decades long relationship, find themselves overcome with laughter one calm afternoon and sounding like the kind of afternoons I want to enjoy for years to come? I think it is their ability to choose love repeatedly. To choose to be kind and patient when your patience is wearing thin. To choose to learn to compromise when selfishness would be an easier choice. Again, not always the easier option and your compromise to accommodate someone should not be at the expense of feeling like you have betrayed yourself and your deepest values. However, you do learn that compromise and loving behaviors are choices you can make.

My son, I hope I haven't lost you in my roundabout kind of way. I want you to hold on to the knowledge that aside from the love of your Creator, you must first accept, appreciate and love yourself. When you learn the value in treating yourself with kindness and patience, you will not only know what that looks like coming from others to you, but you will know how to lead with love when handling others.

I have had to walk the journey of loving myself and still today it is a part of the work I continue to do. I have had to forgive myself, be patient and encouraging to myself and extend all the empathy and care I would to a total stranger to my own heart. I am also learning to love myself well enough to say, "that is not the way to handle this situation." Love also means correction. Once we become the examples of love for ourselves, I believe the rest falls in line.

I love you in such a way I cannot describe but pray in the years to come you will experience my love fully and see me choose loving you even when you have jumped off the edge of my last nerve.

Be love my son.

Start With Gratitude

"Never let your view of your challenges eclipse the view of your blessings" – Marsha Flemmings

I get that for a lot of people who are facing real hardships, it's laughable to hear someone who seemingly doesn't have to deal with the same kinds of problems they do, tell them that they can have more in life if they just express more gratitude. *So you mean that by constantly saying I'm grateful for the air I breathe that I suddenly have more air? Or I suddenly have more money to buy food or pay the rent or survive? Well...mmkay (insert pursed lips and cynical tone).*

A single mother or father who may be struggling financially, sacrificing experiences with their children so they can earn some extra cash may want to be grateful but struggle with seeing through all the bills. There may be a daughter who has suffered through the loss of her mother or father when she is about to start college. The experienced businessman who has been working nearly twenty years in his profession, but can't seem to get the promotion he is working for may struggle with gratitude. A young college graduate with significant student loan debt and is unable to find a job may not know what there is to be grateful for.

Now I could assign things that persons in this scenario could be grateful for. For example, I could say the mother or father could be grateful for healthy children who may be a little disappointed that he or she wasn't at the game, but they understand why. I could also say that the daughter could be happy because she has memories and life lessons that she can hold on to. Truth is, that would be me down playing this practice of gratitude.

Gratitude is a choice! You don't have to practice it. However, just like my opening quote to this chapter suggests, you can either sit with the problems of what is going wrong and why it is so bad that you block out any view of what is going right. Additionally, once you find yourself in that state you are also blocking your view of possibility. There is no fairy dust about this. It is literally the habit of focusing on what you do have with appreciation, no matter how small it seems in comparison to what you want.

Have you ever been having one of those days that almost everything seemed to be going wrong? The car wouldn't start, or you don't have a car in the first place, and it is thunderstorm conditions and you have to get to work. Then when you finally get there, you are late and your boss now wants to have a conversation with you about it because he had a last minute project he needed you to work on and you being late set him back. Maybe at lunch time someone accidentally bumps into you causing you to spill your lunch all over the floor. You finally are making some headway on this last minute project, step away from your desk briefly and return only to discover that you didn't click save so all that work is gone. I think you get the picture. Somewhere in your day, your best friend or spouse reaches out and is trying to cheer you up, but you are in such a bad mood you snap at them and are probably dismissive or said something unkind.

The practice of gratitude doesn't magically make the day's events disappear. However, it can shift your perspective that results in your approach being better and that leads to a decreased sense of frustration or feeling of being overwhelmed. Sometimes the practice of gratitude isn't only about what you have but also positions you to not miss out on something good that is happening because you are fixated on complaining. In this example, if you were able to practice gratitude, appreciation for a friend or partner that is trying to be supportive could result in a lighthearted conversation that helps lift your mood. Instead, what you may now have is someone in your life now upset at you, only making the day that much worse. If your perspective isn't right then it just multiplies the negative. The same is true in reverse.

Liam,

I haven't mastered this and I am relatively new at it because for almost half of my career I was incessantly complaining about some aspect of my job to my friends or family. My frustration with one thing or the other was often on the tip of my tongue. The reality is that I knew I was not passionate about my job and the one aspect of it that I truly enjoyed and felt satisfaction about was the only thing that kept me going for as long as I did. However, there was a time I didn't have that awareness. I wasn't conscious that I really only enjoyed being able to help people, particularly young people discover that they had even more potential than they had acknowledged, that the thing they feared was minute compared to the reward of unlocking all they had in them. The "thank you for helping me", "thank you for believing in me", "because of you I did it" made me feel something that nothing else ever did. During the first half of my career, I wasn't conscious of this.

I grew up seeing both of my parents work hard. My dad often recited, "by the sweat of your brow you shall eat bread." The family had a joke that when my mom went to her job she was actually going home and when she came home to us was where she had to work. We joked, but we believed it because we saw her go a decade without a vacation and none of us believed it was because she couldn't, but she only knew how to throw her whole self at something. My dad was no different. He worked all the time. We saw a bit of each other some mornings while my brother and I got ready for school and he prepared for work. There were many nights he was home after bedtime. From their routine I interpreted that when you have a job you throw your entre being into it, master it and excel.

So naturally when I started a career that would span 17 years, what did I do? I threw myself into it. I stumbled into hospitality. I was job hunting for almost eight months and the job I really wanted informed me that it would be another month or so before they would be ready for me to start training. During my waiting, I received a call from a very successful chain of hotels in the Caribbean. I interviewed, got the job on the spot and asked for two weeks to be able to tie up some business. I was in fact waiting for a call from my dream job.

After a week, the hotel called and said they needed me right away so I went with it. A week into that job my dream job opened up, but I missed the call as I was away for training. In the end, I regret none of it because the company that was offering my dream job at the time did massive downsizing a few months later. The career I ultimately built, the people I have met and all the experiences gained along the way helped to shape me.

The first 9 years of my career I did just as I had seen my parents do. I remember somewhere in my 6th or 7th year and after my third promotion, going six months without one day off. Now the problem with all of this was I wasn't happy doing it, but somehow remained unaware of just how miserable I was at one point. Sure some periods of it was more obvious, like when stress was causing my hair to fallout, but as the years progressed my murmuring and complaining to those I would speak to only became more frequent. This lasted for far too long but eventually and gradually something started to shift. It's hard to explain, but the more I became aware of what I enjoyed about the job, examined what that meant for me, looked at how I could do that more often (which ultimately led to the steps I took to exit that industry), the less I complained. To be clear, those overwhelming feelings never completely disappeared. Like I said, I'm a work in progress. But I definitely realized that the more I focused on what was going right or focused on the aspect of the job that gave me fulfillment, the easier it was to not only continue the job but it ultimately led to me investing the time to research and determine how I could do what I enjoy full time. It led to an amazing year that I challenged myself and set some goals that ultimately prepared me for the next chapter and I believe the gateway to an even more meaningful existence.

This shift could not have happened if my awareness of what I liked, what experience fulfilled me and what felt good didn't happen. Not only did I increase in awareness of those things but I made a conscious effort to be thankful for every time I could participate in that aspect of my job. I also allowed myself to celebrate when I did it well and it yielded the results I hoped for. Outside of the job I enrolled in activities and courses that allowed me to sharpen those skills because I wanted to get even better.

I also arrived at a place where I couldn't help but be thankful for my years of experience in this industry because I believe in many ways that the different circumstances I encountered prepared me on varied levels for what was ahead. All my mistakes, missteps, tense and stressful situations had taught me valuable lessons that better served me in the end.

I could have made my frustrations continue to be my focus and continue with the complaining about my own mistakes or what had not gone right. Believe me, I could have found reasons to complain. I could have complained about being offered a promotion in my latter years that came with more responsibility, but no increase in salary and subsequently not being considered for another opportunity because I declined the first offer. I could complain about being told that since I was starting a family an assumption was made that my approach to work would change so an opportunity was not extended to me. I could sit down and make these things my focus. I could stay in a negative space and beat myself up about every poor decision, missed opportunity or any one thing that didn't go the "ideal" way. That would have cost me so much more time and feeling of unfulfillment and most importantly it would have left me focused on the wrong thing. Every moment spent focusing on the wrong thing is a robbed opportunity to focus on the right thing.

There is a saying that goes, energy flows where attention goes. What I finally understood was that gratitude didn't simply just allow more to fall into your life. What gratitude does is allows you to manage your focus and attention. When you invest more in being in a space where you are aware and mindful of the blessings, the good things, the lessons, it gives you an opportunity to continue to channel that focus and attention in those areas and you inevitably start investing more of yourself in that area. So not only does your perspective shift, but you also naturally start to take more steps in the direction that serves you because it becomes your dominant focus.

Let me suggest an exercise to you that may be helpful in this making sense. Try it with a few people and then ask someone to also try it with you. Find a room, doesn't matter what size. You can strategically place items in the room or they may already be a part of the room already. Invite someone into the space, but before letting them enter the room, give them a goal. For example, they are to find and take out all items made of metal, in as few trips as they possibly can. When they are finished ask them to tell you all the items left in the room that were made of wood, or is the color black, or whatever characteristic suits you. To make it even more interesting you can time them so there is a sense of urgency.

That is just an example, but ultimately what I believe you will find is that they will struggle to give you a list of those things because that was not the focus. Were the things present? Yes. Were they possibly in the way of getting to some of the items they removed from the room? Quite likely. So what would make them not remember these items? Because what you focus on is what gets your attention. To be successful at removing those items in the stipulated time, nothing else can get their focus. Let's say in the process they stop to admire an item that has nothing to do with the task at hand or they simply stop to make an observation, does this have the potential to affect the outcome and their success? Absolutely it does, because they have now shifted their attention from what the task is and are now using valuable time to pay attention to something that doesn't serve them.

Don't get hung up on the item you use in your experiment. You can buy big bags of children's building blocks and ask them to find all the green ones after you have hid all the leggos around the room and then ask them to list all other leggo colors that they found. The point is, what we choose to give our focus is the thing that is going to get our attention and is the thing that we are going to invest our time and energy in. Why not make those things the things that serve us?

I am most thankful for you Liam.

Love Mom.

Fail For The Win

"If you learn from defeat you haven't really lost." – Zig Ziglar

"Failure is the opportunity to begin again more intelligently."– Henry Ford

This topic is so important in my mind that I had to provide an extra quote. I believe it is so important because it is something enough of us don't educate our children about; how to use failure. We sometimes make failure such a bad thing or become so comforting in failure that we often neglect to help children focus on what the failure taught them and how they can use that. Now this is no judgment. We are all in this life experience together and I know many of us do this with the best of intentions. Your child "fails" at something and you comfort them because they feel bad and that's what you are supposed to do right? Or you scold them because you saw it coming, kept on warning them and they didn't heed your warnings. So what else should you do but reinforce to them that this is what you were warning them about and how they could have avoided it if they listened to you? Teach them the value of failure.

Imagine the impact when a child comprehends that while they didn't get the outcome they wanted, these are the things they did or didn't do that led to this outcome. Imagine what happens when they learn that the very experience of failure is what they use to get a better outcome in the future. This mindset may not stick in the first few years. Hell it may not stick until they are in their thirties. The reality is we do more for them by teaching them to look for the lessons in failure as opposed to fearing failure.

Liam,

This lesson is huge Papa and so I hope that you will come to fully understand that in the moments that you failed at something, I wasn't being insensitive about your disappointment. I was simply trying to help you use failure differently than I did in my early years.

A few years ago, I read a book by Napoleon Hill called, Think & Grow Rich. It was loaded with events and the experiences of some pretty successful people who initially experienced setbacks but kept going. The setbacks were not the end of the experience for them. Instead, they used them as opportunities to revisit what was done, what wasn't done and to keep working at it so they could do it better each time until they yielded the outcome they desired.

Around the same time that I first read that book, I also researched some wildly successful people and looked at their own experiences with failure. People like Walt Disney, Steve Jobs, Michael Jordan, Oprah Winfrey, and Henry Ford.

Now why am I suddenly speaking about the experiences of people that you don't even know personally? It's for a couple of reasons.

Firstly, you can learn from anyone, not just those in your immediate sphere or circle. In fact, I encourage you to be *open to learn from everyone and sometimes that means learning what <u>not</u> to do and be which is just as important*

Secondly, and the reason that is at the core of all this, I have allowed fear to cripple me for most of my life up until the point of writing this book and I can't imagine what it has cost me. I too am learning this principle at this stage in my life. I stayed in a career long after I knew it wasn't my passion or my purpose and a big part of what influenced that was fear. Can you imagine my own innate way of overthinking growing 7 heads? What is it that I am meant to be doing? Where will I go? What's the next step? What if it doesn't work out and I ruin my future? Am I capable of taking on a new path that I have no experience in? Will I be taken seriously? Will I earn what I am earning now? Let me tell you that I wished I knew how to make my brain just be quiet!

Do you know what I have realized so far on my own journey with failure? If you risk nothing or try nothing then yes, you can say technically you haven't failed. Do you know what doing that gets you? Absolutely nothing. You stay right where you are with all your dreams, all your desires, all your ambitions and hopes and they die with you. In order to succeed, to achieve anything, you have to take the risk and if the outcome isn't the one you desired then recalculate, learn, adjust, apply and move forward. We are so busy fearing the unknown and failing instead of using the information we have to arm us for it.

Becoming a published author is something I ran away from for years because I feared my writing wasn't good enough, feared that I had nothing valuable to contribute and feared that every inch of my incredibly personal work would be out

55

there for all to criticize. Not to mention that the world has evolved into a place where everyone offers their opinion at every turn in this cyber anonymity plagued experience and my fear crippled me for far too long. I didn't chance anything because I didn't want to fail. I didn't want another experience where I tried something and not have it yield the results I desired. However, the more time passed the more the uneasiness with not pursuing what gave me fulfillment grew and I matured to the place where I decided the fear of failing was a colossal waste of my time. The reality is that I feared something that wasn't even real. It didn't exist except in my mind. What's even worse is that I was risking all the good that could come of pursuing my desires for a possibility that I may not succeed. Truth is not trying at all guarantees failure.

I also really want you to see that even the most successful and influential people fail. None of us are immune to failure. What defines and separates us is how we use failure. I could tell you the stories I read on how Walt Disney was told he had no creativity and imagination by a previous employer and even went on to run an animation studio into bankruptcy before building the empire that he did. A Baltimore TV producer told Oprah Winfrey she was "unfit for television news." Can you imagine? Look at what she has manifested. A gentleman by the name of Steve Jobs co-founded a company called Apple and he was let go from the company and it was very public. You can research him and see how he then co-founded another company that would ultimately be acquired by Apple and when he rejoined it, he ushered in a new wave of innovation that took over the market. The phenomenon that is Michael Jordan has shared his early setbacks when he wasn't picked for his University's basketball team and the work he had to do to improve his performance. He could have stopped there. He could have let that temporary setback become his permanent story. Oh how the game of basketball would have missed one of its greatest stars.

Again, this isn't to exalt any public figure. I only want you to get that what separates greatness from mediocrity in any aspect of life and with anyone is how we experience and process "failures" and subsequently how we use the information that the experience can teach us.

So on that note, fail often, fail forward, fail for the win.

I love you my son.

Money Mindset

**"Money does not change people. It unmasks them." –
Unknown**

Multiple surveys show that money is one of the top three
causes for the dissolution of marriages. So we know we are
walking into some pretty serious territory here. As much as a
part of me was inclined to leave out his particular subject
matter, I came to my senses and recalled that the whole point
of this book is to engage in a discussion about matters that
parents don't always make the time to discuss or address with
children. The prevailing thought appears to be that if it does
not come up in the traditional spheres of education, then it is
not important enough to be addressed.

Now my bank account will be the first to tell you that you
aren't talking to a millionaire, yet! My account will also tell
you that she's been growing and will continue to grow. Of all
the lessons that I've been consciously working through, my
relationship with money has become one of the most
important ones. It's no coincidence that this interest, focus and
attention to my beliefs and behaviors concerning money
heightened significantly after the birth of my son. In fact, it
grew exponentially while I was pregnant with him.

During the process of writing this book, I was in Bali headed
to a theatre and happened on a little bookstore. Among the 6
books I walked out with was a book by Robert Kiyosaki, *Rich
Dad Poor Dad*. I encourage every human being to read it. I'm

not saying that so you can simply adopt one human beings point of view as your own. More than anything, I want us all to read it so it provokes our own thoughts and memories to determine what we learned about money. Who did we learn it from? Did those lessons serve us or sabotage us? How can I change what I want to change about my relationship with money? You don't necessarily need the book to help you ask and answer these questions, but the contrasting experiences offered in the book were an interesting duality to read about and was truly thought provoking.

Dear Liam,

Young Pa and G. Ma were both professional working class people who, at the time, were raising a young family and were mindful of money because they were always saving to do home improvements, or for the kids' education, or for travel, or for something important in the future. While I believe they had the same mission, I definitely know that Young Pa was also a big believer in living and enjoying the present. He didn't believe in living only for tomorrow which also meant that he was willing to spend in some scenarios when G. Ma would rather put the money up and prepare for the apocalypse. Similarly, when it came to investments, Young Pa was the risk taker. G. Ma wanted no parts of anything other than securing her money in a savings or fixed account. So these two approaches, unknown to me, were influencing my relationship with money along with other experiences I would have.

I have a few early memories about money. One of the earliest being your uncle and me heading to a cookout at church one afternoon only to discover that our money was missing by the time we arrived. We searched every inch of the 10 minute walk from the church back to the house and didn't find it. My heart was pounding and I was stressed to think I lost money. We weren't poor, but I certainly didn't experience your grandparents throwing money away.

When we made it back home, I don't recall G. Ma being upset which made it worse because what I thought was that she was disappointed. I remember walking to my room kneeling beside the bed and praying. I'm pretty sure I was in the middle of striking a deal with God, maybe offering a bribe is more accurate, when I heard the voice of a stranger at the front door. This man had stopped by. He told my mom that he was driving and noticed something in the middle of the street. He turned around to see what it was and realized it was money. He looked around for a while and didn't see anyone until he noticed your uncle and I heading down the street. He said he watched us and that's how he ended up at our home. I don't even remember if I went back to the cookout. What I remember was feeling relieved that I hadn't just thrown money away.

Among my other early memories are seeing my mother establish a monthly budget, my dad giving mom money at the end of each month to cover bills and some just for her, or being told about tithing, or being given my money for lunch for the week and having to learn discipline to ensure I wasn't starving at school by Wednesday. Equally as important as what I saw was what I heard. My mom would often say, "I can't afford it." Looking back in most, if not all cases, she could have afforded it, but chose not to or prioritized more important things. The point is she often spoke from a place of awareness or concern for lack or limitation and sometimes my dad did the same. I don't believe this happened consciously. They were just two people who had created a family that they were insistent on providing as much as they possibly could for and that meant money had to be managed properly and not wasted.

During the summers of my college years, I worked with a wholesale travel company in Pennsylvania. One summer, I was running a bit late to catch my flight to head back home. The flight was very early in the morning so there was less activity to contend with in my haste. I made it through just in the nick of time. The second I sat in my seat I remembered that

I had left my pocketbook on the belt at the security checkpoint. I ran back and as I approached, a smiling officer walked up to me and confirmed what I knew to be true. I thanked her profusely and darted quickly in the direction of my gate. Seated again, I exhaled, tilted my head back and thought how fortunate I was to get it back without incident. The moment I had the thought, I had a sinking feeling in my gut. I immediately opened the pocketbook to see if the over $1000 dollars in cash I had was still there. I could not believe my eyes. $23. That's all that was there. I closed the pocketbook, shook my head and thought for a second before opening it again with the belief that I was just being hysterical and the funds were all there and I just didn't see it. Well! It still wasn't there. I searched the other compartments of the pocketbook knowing fully well it wasn't there. Now there was a whole saga that ensued thereafter when I brought the matter to the attention of the flight attendant and told her I just needed a few minutes to get off the plane because they had stolen all the money I had saved up that summer.

I cried the first part of the flight and there was a lovely flight attendant who not only moved me up to first class that day but took the time to talk to me and one thing she said was, "Don't worry. One day you will make that money back and much more and you won't miss it." In the moment it wasn't a truth I could accept, but it made a lasting impression on me. While I was still hurt and disappointed, by the end of the flight I had decided that it was already done. I had to head home as a new school year was starting and life had to go on. We would see what investigation could be done but I had to accept that this was the reality. Relatively quickly, I was able to shift my perspective and decide not to attach any anxiety, stress or negative energy to money. I had lost it. It was gone. Moping wasn't going to bring it back.

The same thing happened when a guy I dated years later, who was eight years my senior, borrowed nearly $ 4, 000 to help his failing business. I should have known better and my instincts tried to warn me, but young, dumb and dating has no cure. It took me a little longer this time around because I started the process of filing a claim against him. Then I reminded myself that I would not attach anxiety, stress or negative energy to my thoughts and feelings concerning money. I also told myself exactly what that flight attendant told me what would have been more than 6 years before.

So when he didn't return my money and a few years later reached out to me unexpectedly, saying he was calling to get his woman back and resolve the loan, I laughed. It wasn't my intention to, but that was my honest reaction. The truth is by the time he had called back I was already making twice the amount of money I was earning while we were dating and was on the verge of another promotion. I remember when it all had just happened, telling myself that the day will come where I will blink and make that money. So this impromptu call had little to no meaning to me and I was able to end the call wishing him the best and not wanting or needing anything from him, including the money. At the end of the call I felt power in that moment, knowing that I truly was able to release any anxiety, pain or anger relating to him or the money he owed me.

Don't misunderstand; I made my mistakes in those situations. I rushed through the airport. In retrospect, I did not organize myself in a way that ensured I wouldn't lose something. I walked away from the machine without ensuring I had what was mine. I also loaned money to a man who signaled more than enough red flags to tell me I shouldn't have. Those were my choices and there were lessons to learn in them as well.

I had to learn that my money deserves my attention and to be in control of where my money goes means I need to have it organized and secured. Otherwise, it will end up in the hands of those who I don't intend to have it. I had to learn that I should not be reckless concerning what I do with my money, no matter how much or how little of it I have. I also decided that I had to be smarter in relationships. Well, take my brain along for the ride in the first place. I grew to understand that my heart was made to love and my brain was made to think and I should not confuse the two. There were many lessons but for sure I have held onto the belief that what serves me is to attach positive emotions to money.

In more recent times, your arrival triggered a rush of thoughts and emotions about ensuring I am always in a financial position to set you up to win and I worked consciously to keep those emotions in check. The legacy I am mindful to work at building for you obviously goes beyond finances, hence these letters, but a strong financial legacy is also on the list. Teaching you about money is critical. In the culture I grew up in, parents didn't often invest in that facet of a child's knowledge and the result of it has been very damaging.

I have decided that starting in your early years I will place you in environments and in the presence of people who you can learn from but until then let me offer my own suggestions:

- *Who you are has nothing to do with your bank account. However what is in your bank account can amplify who you are. So I encourage you that the greatest work of your life must be on yourself.*
- *Money is not evil. How we feel about money and what we become willing to do for it is where we introduce a problem to the equation.*
- *Money is not evil. How we feel about money and what we become willing to do for it is where we introduce a problem to the equation.*
- *Educate yourself about money mindset and management or at minimum solicit the assistance of someone that has, that also has a genuine interest in your success in this area*
- *Money is a medium of exchange. You exchange it for your needs and wants: the products, the experiences and the conveniences. In your exchanges you are still leading with your values and that will dictate what you trade it for.*
- *Invest. Take a chance. Risk. Just take informed risks. Risk early.*
- *I believe in the practice and discipline of tithing. Simply put, I was created by a superior being. I call my life force God. Without Him creating me and providing all that I need, I would have nothing and giving back to Him is my duty.*
- *The power of compound interest can change your life.*
- *Give freely and with good intent.*
- *Decide from all your earnings what you will save (I use that word loosely) and make that a habit. A common recommendation is 15%. I say shoot for a*

minimum of 30%. Your future, retired early, travelling the world and living your best life self will thank me.

- [ ] *Money cannot, will not and can never bring happiness. Happiness is an inside job, so don't seek it outside of yourself.*

Make that money my son. Don't let it make you.

Mommy

The Fight for Forgiveness.

"The weak can never forgive. Forgiveness is an attribute of the strong." Mahatma Gandhi

So here is the thing, as with anything else, how you choose to hold on to the anger, the pain and the hurt of someone who has done "wrong" to you is as much your choice as how you exercise faith or what you believe love is. It's all a choice.

As parents, guardians, aunts, uncles, foster parents, social workers, whomever, we have our own principles on all these matters. Yes, it would be easier to just assume our way has been the best way to handle all these things and then consciously or unconsciously pass these lessons on to the generations to come.

Let me ask you to consider though that maybe there is another way that could yield different outcomes, possibly more favourable ones. Should that be the case, how willing are we to explore those avenues not just for ourselves but for our children, so that maybe they have a better experience than we had?

So a friend has hurt you, a colleague has betrayed you, a family member has used you or a child has disappointed you. Stop for a moment and consider how you handle those discoveries? How long do you hold on to the emotion before addressing it? Did you ever address it with them? After you have addressed it, do you still hold on to those feelings? How has your way of being in these circumstances served you? Did it ultimately change or cost you a relationship that you could have salvaged that was worth salvaging? Did you evaluate or consider if you were culpable in the situation? If so, did you acknowledge it. When you were able to release any negative energy from a situation, how did you do it and what helped?

These questions aren't meant to make you wrong or right. They are meant to help you stop and think and fully recognize your mode of operating, to evaluate the outcomes of this approach and determine if those are the values you believe will best serve your next generation.

Dear Liam,

You get to decide who you are in this world. No one else! However, what will happen is your relationships will no doubt present circumstances that will test you and your integrity regarding who you say you are. I would desire, as any other parent would I am sure, to be able to have you learn life's lessons void of any hurt or disappoint or your own mistakes. That's just not how it works and on top of that I believe you can't fully show up and become that person without the character building experiences that lead to evolution.

So who will you be when it concerns forgiving others and acknowledging your own mistakes?

I suspect that this may be my shortest letter to you and I believe that to be for a very specific reason. Forgiveness, while difficult to work through at times, is a simple choice.

There is immense simplicity in it when we are able to think of it void of our emotions.

What do I mean? There's a simple way to look at this. Someone punches you in the gut and knocks the wind out of you and as a result you decide to hold your breath and no longer breathe. What happens? Ummmmm... this is a no brainer. You die. What's worse is you chose to die. You chose to die because of what someone else did to you?

So let's strip away the dramatics and look at it a bit more practically. The gut punch represents whatever action someone took that hurt, disappointed or angered you. You couldn't help it. It was their actions. Your response or feeling towards the action is in the wind being knocked out of you. You also can't help but feel that. That reaction comes naturally. Now after the moment where you become aware of the pain and the wind being gone, you have a choice; to start breathing and figuring out how to soothe the pain.

The reality is so many of us get stuck right in the moment of the gut punch and we live the next 10, 20 or 40 years behaving like the gut punch just happened.

Did it hurt? Yes! Was it unexpected? Yes! Were you in pain? Yes! Was the breath knocked out of you? Yes! Can you start breathing again after being bent over in pain? Yes! Can you then try to soothe the pain or take a moment for the pain to subside? Absolutely!

Believe me, I am not trying to trivialize disappointment or betrayal. However, what I want to help you avoid is you getting stuck with it for the rest of your life knowing that you have a choice.

I hope the thought that "forgiveness is not for the other person, it is for you" is something you can process early on in life. Keeping anger, malice, hurt and unforgiveness keep you stuck. Your growth and evolution are limited if you don't let those things go. You will be trying to continue your journey through this life with the weight of the anger you have towards your betrayal. That weight will cause you to draw on more energy than you would have to use, had you just freed yourself. Crazily, in some situations those who are unwilling to choose to forgive carry on with so much awareness of their pain for so many years and they allow it to influence so many decisions they make, while the person who betrayed them has moved on and carried on not allowing themself to be held back by the weight of not releasing the experience.

I mentioned before that it can be complex to work through, but allow yourself to do the work. Feel the emotion, be aware of it and then do the work to heal yourself. Notice I am not selling you on a notion that every situation you will simply experience the betrayal and in the seconds to follow you simply throw it away and say, "I have forgiven you." Many of those experiences will require you to confront hard facts and strong emotions. I'm just challenging you for the benefit of your spirit and the benefit of your ability to grow without anything holding you back. I want you empowered to choose forgiveness despite how you feel you have been wronged.

Though forgiveness is presented to us as a choice I desire that you grow to a place where you don't give yourself an option but to forgive, because you would have learned that who you choose to be in this life, accomplishing all that you are capable of, living and being at your maximum capacity and potential does not deserve to be held captive by your anger, hurt or disappoint.

I pray you always choose to release yourself.

Love you my son.

The Journey Has A Purpose

"I am learning to trust the journey even when I do not understand it." - Mila Bron

Some of the darkest times in our lives can really have us feeling lost, afraid, alone and confused. While we are all made up differently, the reality is that the loss of a loved one, the failure of a business that you invested everything in, the dissolution of a marriage, the diagnosis of a life threatening disease, you name it. Anyone of those things can have us feeling completely outside of ourselves. Your center, any clarity of thought and any strength you knew yourself to have can, in those moments, completely disappear.

In those moments, very often, we are more aware of our emotional response to what is happening than what we know, or on what we are meant to be learning. That's human. However, how do we not just "pick up the pieces and go on", but hold on to the knowledge that in every experience, painful or otherwise, there is a lesson, a reminder... something that we can take away. It may sound overly simplistic, but when we move beyond emotion we can get some work done. This doesn't mean we don't acknowledge the presence of those emotions, but we don't need to live in it forever and ever amen. Think about it. Don't you find that when the emotions somehow become less dominant or pronounced, you are able to move in the direction of what you know?

The intention of this letter to my son is to help him understand that both the sunshine and the rain feed us and one without the other cannot provide all we need to thrive. In fact, if you think of a plant, the rain feeds its roots and helps the growth to happen starting below the surface. This speaks to your foundation, your core. You can connect that to your character, your guiding beliefs, who you are. Then the process of photosynthesis happens after the plant has already grown and has leaves. The sunlight is what they use to help feed themselves, but growth had to have already taken place for there to be leaves. When the seed is buried in the darkness and the water is poured on it creating those dark and damp experiences, that entire experience is pulling those things out of the seed and helping it take root, so that it continues to grow and evolve. All that the tree will become is grounded in this process.

I believe our lives are similar. It is through the hard experiences that our roots are pulled out of us, that what is on the inside of us is being summoned to expose itself. Remember that these experiences will be dark and lonely conditions. Many times while having these experiences there is no glimmer of the sunlight for a while. Without the knowledge that the experience is happening for the purpose of pulling something out of us, creating a learning that will help us break the surface, grow, produce leaves and fruit, then we will remain in the darkness with our form unchanged.

Dear Liam,

I want you to know and be clear that I have not lived a perfect life. I've been hurt, disappointed, mistreated, misjudged and taken advantage of. I have also disappointed people, misjudged people, been selfish and sometimes made poor choices. For any of us, whether these things happen intentionally or not isn't what's most important. What is important is what we take from the situation, like "What did I learn about that person?" or "What did I learn about myself?" and ultimately "How do I use all that the experience is able to teach me for my ultimate good?"

I'm sharing this because I want you to know that while I encourage you to be the best possible version of yourself, to live life full out, to have faith, be strong, to love, be grateful, build relationships and all that is good, I also have to tell you that many life experiences will be tough. Some will feel dark and possibly lonely. I want you to know that you will have experiences that feel like they are designed to break you but they are simply pulling something out of you.

What's more important is that I want you to be prepared to take from them what they are meant to give you. Often, as humans going through a tough experience, we draw into solitude and self-pity. We lash out in anger or move in denial. Each experience is offering us something. Sometimes we are being redirected because we are heading in the wrong direction. Sometimes the experience is offering us an opportunity to grow, cultivate some more patience, learn how to love, operate with more integrity and honesty or simply discover our own strength. I have found that tough times are teaching us a lesson that we need to learn or it will keep showing up until we do.

When I was twenty years old, my first job after I graduated was going better than I could have imagined. I had received awards from the company in my first three months and a promotion by the fifth month. I was called into a meeting to discuss the company's plans for me. They intended to put me through a two year training program to prepare me to head up their Sales division. The training included time in their finance department, the warehouse and distribution division and time with the Outside Sales Managers, as I was already familiar with inside Sales. I couldn't be more humbled and excited. Two of my best girlfriends today, I met on that job. I initially felt some concern for how they may take it because we had just forged friendships. I joined the company sometime after them and was being promoted. However, I was always so uncertain of myself and made a habit of questioning the value that I bring to anything that this promotion really provided a validation that I thought I needed.

During this transition we received a new manager. She seemed okay initially, but I distinctly remember the day she became aware of the plans for me and remember thinking that her approach to me had changed. It was nothing overly obvious or mean, but there was a difference. There was just this arm's length distance and disconnect. It could have had nothing to do with me, but it seemed a little coincidental.

One morning, my friends stopped by my house and we left for work together. I drove on to the complex with them driving on behind me. I parked at the front of the property and as I walked in they slowed down to ask me to punch their time cards. They were parking at the back of the property where the warehouse was located. So I walked in, and punched all three time cards.

Just before lunch the manager asked to meet with me. She queried if I punched in any time card other than my own. I said yes. Even in that moment I don't believe I understood that would have been a concern. However, her face and tone made it very clear that it was a problem. She asked if I was aware that I should not punch anyone else's time card. I apologized and told her, in my naivety, that I thought there wouldn't be a problem as they were physically here. I wasn't sneaky or hiding when I punched their cards because back then, I did not get why this would be a concern. Before the day was done I was fired. When I returned to the office to get my belongings and everyone asked where I was going, no one believed when I said I was just fired. I was literally through the front door when they came outside to confirm what was going on.

I didn't know how to make sense of what had transpired and it took me years to mature to the understanding that the outcome of that day was on me. It wasn't as a result of anyone else's actions but my own. For far too long I entertained the thought of how could a company see so much potential in someone and make such a drastic decision? They could easily verify everything I said. There was surveillance all over the premises. I gave so much time practicing one of the biggest mistakes I believe we make as human beings. So often we criticize the reaction or response from others to the things that we do, instead of looking at our actions that created the response. That alone robs us of so much learning and keeps us stuck where we are. That is where I stayed for a few years in my mind.

It took me eight months before I was hired for another job. Those eight months included a lot of stress, crying, job hunting and contemplation. I remember having dark circles appear all over my back and arms which the doctor advised was as a result of the stress I was holding on to. What I later discovered was that the job had provided this validation I thought I needed. It gave me some kind of purpose and direction. I was looking for something outside of myself that I could only find inside me. It took time for that discovery because I was still very young.

This new job resulted in a 17 year career. The first half of that career I averaged a promotion every 18 months. The second half I guided a record amount of team members to some of the most prestigious awards in our company. My promotions led to me working in new countries and an even broader experience than I believe I would have gotten before I lost my first job. The journey wasn't all smooth but it helped me learn so much about myself and the evolution that ultimately occurred came from all the experiences that came through this 17 year journey.

After I was fired, it almost felt like everything was falling apart. I felt such pain and turmoil about not knowing where my life was going, which was especially hard for a personality like mine that feels a need to plan everything. I felt so lost and youthful ignorance contributed to me not understanding that life goes on, you learn, pick up the pieces and move forward. I smile at my distress back then because little did I know that the road ahead held so much more than the road I had already travelled. The road ahead also included meeting your dad which brought you into both our lives, in one of the countries that a promotion brought me to.

So by trusting the process what I hope you get is that the process often times is painful and takes you through some experiences that you would rather not have. I made my own mistakes. I should have handled some things so much better. I contributed to my own pain but it was all a part of the process of me growing. So when you are buried in the soil and it is not the ideal situation, in fact it is downright uncomfortable and painful, that is because something is being pulled out of you that is going to produce something beyond what you can see in that moment. Never worry because the crack of sunlight will soon come through.

I love you with everything in me.

Your Mommy.

The Legacy of A Man

"If boys don't learn, men won't know" - Douglas Wilson

Before you start laughing that I, a woman, would attempt to explain to my son what it is like to be a man or what it means to be a man, hear me out. That's actually not what I'm about to do.

I heard a few times, "A man is who his mother makes him to be." I didn't accept that for some time as I didn't understand it nor did I connect with the truth in it until recently. The legacy of a man is being shaped long before he becomes a man. In fact, scientific research says that when a pregnant woman has thoughts that evolve into emotions, those feelings and emotions cause her body to release chemicals that can affect multiple things in an unborn baby including brain development. So from the very beginning a woman's ability to manage stress, diet and overall health before, during and after pregnancy plays a role.

I know that your child, my child and all children are never affected or shaped only by one thing, one person or one experience. Yes, someone can have more significant impact or a particular experience can create more of a change in a child than another experience. There are so many things that shape children including their own innate tendencies.

However, generally with women, the nurturing of children, the nurturing of the home even, is a fundamental part of what we offer. In the case of a boy child, she is offering something that is said to not be an aspect of him that is generally pronounced.

I am not speaking to traditional roles in the home or any of that. What I am referring to is our genetic makeup. As women, we nurture. The life is formed, shaped and developed in us. The very physiological design of breastfeeding supports that fact. A mother introduces the concept of nurturing to her son. So if she reinforces only his innate and genetic tendencies then she doesn't challenge or expand his perspective. If she is not supporting him in developing a healthy way to express and handle his emotions, then she is only reinforcing what his make-up and the rest of society will tell him about those emotions. I am speaking very generally of course, because we have families where a mother is absent and I will not suggest that a man cannot nurture his child. I have seen many fathers live this experience.

Ultimately this is about how your 2 year old, 10 year old and 16 year old son will show up in this world as a man. Will he be in tune with his emotions or taught to suppress them? Will he understand his role as a man with a woman? Will he grasp the significance of his role in his family? Will he know that while you should be protecting and serving, it is okay to be served and to allow appreciation to flow through his life? Will he understand that he was created by a superior being and cultivating that relationship will also influence and shape him? How will he view his role in society? Will he understand that he is not only required to be strong in a healthy relationship, but that his vulnerability is safe in the presence of a woman who knows how to love him? Who is he being nurtured to become?

Dear Liam,

Should this be your desire, I would only pray for you to experience the joys that come with loving a woman, building a family and a home with her. However, who you will be to that woman, that family and in society is already a person that is taking shape. In fact, I believe your ability to be on that journey and be clear on who that man is before walking into that woman's life, or creating that family is going to be of more service to you.

It was no surprise to me that shortly before you turned two years old, never having sat at a keyboard, you sat in front of your cousin's keyboard and positioned your hands and fingers in such a way that your grandmother remarked it was exceptional for a child at that stage. Music was one of the main things I used to sustain our connection during pregnancy. I would take a portable speaker into the bathroom when I showered, playing music while I danced. After a while it was reduced to a sway, holding my belly and allowing the water to beat down on it. I wanted to nurture, if science was right, your inclination towards music.

It was also with intention that I went with you on daily walks. In the mornings we would stand by the ocean and pray. In the evenings we would go for a stroll along the road or on a nearby golf course. It was with the same intention that before you could speak I would sit with you on the living room floor and do flashcards with you. I was trying to nurture your sense of awareness that not only are we a part of a bigger world but that there was a force that was so much larger than us and that we are divinely connected to Him. I was attempting to encourage you to speak and identify the things around you.

81

See as your mother while other things crossed my mind, I spent so much time consciously thinking of how much attention I would give you, how I would engage with you, how I could help encourage your sense of curiosity and wonder. I was nurturing you. I was in my own way encouraging you and gently challenging you to move your evolution along because I knew these things were inside you. I knew it would not all happen at once. However, I believed I should continuously expose you to these things and nurture what I knew you would become, instead of just speaking to your current state.

Naturally, your dad would have a different set of thoughts. Not better, not worse, just different. His daily thoughts and focus would have to do with ensuring that he was always able to provide for and protect you. That just seems to be the natural inclination of the human adult male.

Along this journey, I will have to be conscious of how I encourage you to process your own thoughts, feelings and emotions. I am aware that I cannot teach you all your life that boys are not supposed to cry but then expect that you magically become a man capable of expressing his emotions effectively when I would have been teaching you to suppress them. The same is true for any emotion. You are allowed to own them. What I believe I need to help you cultivate is the ability to process them in such a way that serves you instead of harms you.

There are some things I know you will only learn and truly understand after having your own experiences. However, that doesn't negate my responsibility to share with you what I have come to understand in my 38 years of being in this life. So you can have your own experiences, learn from them and maybe learn from a few of the things your wise mother told you (wink wink).

Again, it's never my intention to live for you but who among us sees someone we love and care for walking into a lion's den and not at least say in warning that, "the lion is the big hairy animal with the teeth as big as your head?"

I simply want to introduce you to the concept of living consciously from as early as you can. Being open to the understanding that whatever you create is going to represent what you have to offer. So what you create in love, with family, professionally, financially can only be a representation of where you are and who you are. Chaos cannot produce clarity. Insecurity cannot produce certainty. Arrogance cannot produce humility. Inconsistency cannot produce change.

This is the knowledge that if you discover early can change your life. It is life changing because it impacts how you treat yourself, how you treat others, how you handle the mountain tops and the valleys.

After welcoming you into my life, not only did family take on an even greater meaning to me, but the awareness that who I am was now going to shape and influence who you would become was something that drove me into an even deeper self-discovery. Greater still was the rediscovery that who I am always offered the capability to shape and influence others, not just my own child. That is our legacy. The ripple effects of our actions go further than we can see and those effects will outlive us. I encourage you to be clear in your vision of who you are and the kind of ripple effects you will create that will outlive you. I love you Liam.

You Own Your I Am

"Your opinion of me doesn't define who I am " – Unknown

One of the things I wish I had come to know much earlier in my life is that I have ownership of who I become and who I say I am. It sounds like such a simple thing, but I have discovered that more people than I ever imagined come to this realization much later in life than they would have preferred to. Think about it. How many people do you know didn't do something, go somewhere, date someone, wear a piece of clothing, fix their hair or makeup a particular way because of what someone thought or what they believed someone would think? They didn't pursue their dream because someone thought they weren't smart enough, or pretty enough or that they didn't have the resources to do it.

I know many people that have had the struggle of others around them telling them who they are, if they are good enough, what they can be and what they can do. I have met many whose families, colleagues, spouses, teachers or even friends tell them they couldn't be or do something. Many of us allow that to happen to us, we choose to believe what other people say about us, or the fear of what we think others will say about us to influence who we are.

My experience was a little different. The voice I constantly heard telling me how unworthy I was, or why I couldn't achieve something was my own. I was fortunate to have friends and family that were predominantly supportive and encouraging. I met people along the way through work, different organizations that I was a part of, mentors and people I mentored who believed that I had way more potential than what I had manifested up until the point they met me. I was seldom, if ever, met with a negative word about my capabilities from those around me. So why didn't I know this very thing with the degree of certainty that they did?

You and I literally can decide that we want to be a person of integrity, courage, resilience, patience and any other attribute and the power is within us to cultivate those qualities if we do not innately possess them. It took me many years of introspection and evaluating my self-talk and limiting beliefs and then the real work began. I had to start the work of changing that chatter and managing my fear. I had to forgive myself for my mistakes and figure out what each mistake and experience was teaching me. I did not want to be held captive by any limiting belief, be it the voice of a loved one, a stranger, or the voice in my head.

Dear Liam,

As far back as I can remember I was so concerned with my place, my role, if I fit in, if I was "acceptable" or simply enough. I cringe to think of how much I desired to feel like I belonged, that I was enough and that nothing was wrong with me.

It may have started before this, but I definitely remember this feeling in high school. I was a member of several clubs, held a few leadership roles in some initiatives at the school and was one of four girls selected to do a student exchange with North

Atlanta High School. While our school was well esteemed in our community, relative to North Atlanta High School, my high school in Jamaica's second city was smaller, so this was a big deal. Despite what I was involved in and how well any of it went, or how well I did, I somehow always felt either out of place or somehow not as good as the rest.

I think I may have some more digging to do to unearth where this constant self-doubt and comparison to others came from. What I do know is that I was riddled with feelings of inadequacy and it may not have always appeared that way to others because I made a lot of effort to appear confident and well put together. If from the start I didn't think I could do something, chances are I wasn't going to try it because the last thing I wanted to do was have the attention of others and look silly. I had done that epically when I was in the 6th grade and entered a talent competition at school. I don't know what made me think I could sing, and a Whitney Houston song no less. I am laughing now, but cringed for years when I think of me squealing that last note and ending to a lone person clapping in an audience of a few hundred. That one person may have been your uncle. I was not prepared to make that mistake in life again.

I have your Young Pa to thank for working to reinforce a strong sense of self because had it not been for some of those conversations we had, when I got older and was trying to evaluate it all, I don't know how I would have clarified some of the thoughts in my head.

We once were attending a very popular pageant. I remember we arrived late and met a crowded ballroom, most chairs filled and people standing at the back. When we opened the door to that ballroom, the show had just started, the only seats that we saw were on the opposite side of the room and the only clear path to get there was between the front row and the stage. So I turned and pointed the seats out to my dad and asked him how are we going to get there and he asked what I meant. So I pointed out the only route I could see without having to maneuver our way through a crowd. So he motioned for me to start walking and I hesitated. I remember this expression on his face that suggested he didn't understand my hesitation. He simply said, "Do you think there is anyone here better than you? There isn't. We are all just people. So hold your head up, walk across the room and let's find some seats."

My teenage brain didn't get it then but without recognizing it at first, that experience stayed with me and almost two decades later was something that I used to ground myself whenever I found myself choosing to shrink in the presence of others. I reminded myself that we all are just people.

In my adulthood, I had to own that I allowed myself to shrink in the presence of others. I somehow convinced myself that because they either had more money, or attended a better school, or lived in a particular community that they somehow were better people.

I discovered the truth eventually though my love. That is, we are all flawed. There is beauty and imperfection in us all. More importantly, this life isn't about comparison as it robs you of your purpose and distracts you from a powerful truth. Standing yourself next to another and determining what they have that you don't or what you have they lack, in that moment takes away your power to see how what you have can serve you even better where you are, or best yet, serve others.

Let the person you constantly look at and measure be yourself because that is the only person you will ever have complete ownership of. When you do measure and assess yourself, don't shy away from the broken parts of yourself. Many times the beauty in life comes from healing those broken parts.

There is a Japanese art form, Kintsugi, in which breaks and cracks in ceramics are carefully mended with gold or silver mixed into a resin. The breaks and cracks are beautifully obvious. Our own life experiences can be the same. We don't have to believe that it is over for us or that our worth is diminished because of our cracks, chips and flaws. In fact, if we know how to heal those things, they not only serve us and serve the world, but somehow make our contribution more meaningful. Imagine that. The things we sometimes feel shame about can become the things that increase our value.

You get to decide and not another. There's a saying I heard of some time ago and I don't know where it originated but it says, "It's not what the world calls you, but what you answer to that matters." So understand that when I say you own "your I am", it doesn't mean you will be perfect, nor does it mean it will be easy. It simply means you decide.

My father did a lot in my early years to reassure me of my value. However, it wasn't until I could make sense of that and could believe that for myself did it change my life. Irrespective if it comes from someone being critical or from a loved one assuring you of what they think your capabilities are, know that what is even more important is who you say you are.

While you are at it, I encourage you to dare to be great. I dare you to be the best version of yourself.

I look forward to seeing the man that you will decide to become.

I love every part of you.

Mommy

What's the Right Thing To Do?

My Dear Son,

I am sure you will be nodding your head, as you read this statement with the painful familiarity of having heard me say it in real life at least a million times…well, I'm your mom and I'm supposed to annoy you with "wise sayings" until you understand the wisdom in them.

"ALWAYS do the right thing."

Sometimes the right thing to do won't necessarily be the right thing for you. It won't even always be easy or be the option that is staring you in the face. Sometimes you will hear your deepest inner voice quietly nudging you in that direction; though that is the last thing you want to do. However, in becoming the man of integrity you are created to be, the strength to do the right thing in any given situation is a strength you will have to learn to call upon. Living a life of someone of worth isn't in the value of your house, your car, or the money in the bank or any material possession or who you know. Be mindful of anyone who only appreciates you for having those things. Those things are nice to have but they are not who you are.

So what defines who you are? You are defined by your words, your actions and how those two things are consistent with each other. How you treat others, especially those that may not be able to do anything for you. How you treat yourself. Do you honor your word? Does what you say match what you do? Do you acknowledge and take ownership of your mistakes? Or do you make the tragic mistake too many of us make and blame others where we need to take responsibility? What do you believe? What do you believe about yourself? What do you think is possible? Are you consistent? Are you growing? What is your contribution?

When there is an absence of consistency between your words and your actions or your beliefs and your actions you erode your integrity. You also ultimately erode your relationship with yourself because each time you don't honor your word, or who you say you are, you are teaching yourself that you will not show up and do the right thing. Let's say you have a friend and each time they say they will be there they don't show up for you. You eventually get to a place where you don't trust them to show up, you question their loyalty to you and the love they say they have for you. The relationship you build with yourself is the same.

I've learned that my words are so important and that I have responsibility for them and believe me it took me way too long to get this. The example I have been using for a few years now is if I am speaking to my closest friend about something someone else did that angered or frustrated me and those words come back to face me in the presence of the person I was speaking about, I must be able to own those words. Now was I speaking to a trusted friend and confidant? Yes. Is what I share in that space private? Yes. May it be emotionally charged and blunt? Yes. Would I have wanted it to be expressed to the person I was speaking about in that way? No. But are they my words? Yes. Is it right to own that I said them? Absolutely! That's been a huge lesson for me.

I had an associate that had trusted me with some personal information, as he had done before. It was pretty significant to him. A few days later a friend of mine was having a conversation with me and had said a few things that led me to believe she knew the information and I engaged in the conversation. He later queried how she had access to the information and though I knew I had not been the one to tell her, when he asked if I had said anything, I was initially tempted to deny it. However, this question that I had gotten in the habit of asking myself just would not let me live in peace. Without making any excuses, I owned the conversation exactly as it went.

What happened from that was so profound to me, because I thought for sure I had ruined his confidence in me. However, because I said to him that I couldn't walk away knowing I had a conversation and allow him to believe I didn't and I just had to do the right thing, he developed even more respect and trusted me with even more critical matters in his life for years to follow. Let me tell you, the shame of having to own that to him was real, but I didn't do it to save the relationship. In fact, I could have walked away without owning it because my friend came to me knowing the information. However, I knew that the relationship I had built with myself about doing the right thing would suffer. I would not at all be proud of myself.

By that time, I had been, guiding young people to live with integrity and owning their stuff. How could I go home, have dinner and go to bed not doing the same? There was no nobility in it. This was purely me holding myself accountable for what I believed. From all indications I could have walked away without speaking the truth and there would have been no consequence and nothing to lose, except the respect and confidence I had built in myself to do the right thing. This is what I mean in expressing that the right thing may not always seem like it is in your best interest or in some situations may seem inconsequential, but the correlation between who you say you are and the daily actions you take to demonstrate that will build more in you than I can explain.

Saying you are sorry when you are wrong, owning your stuff and acknowledging your shortcomings will not kill you. In fact, you will find that some may ultimately respect you and appreciate your honesty and more importantly the person you become in the process is someone that you will be proud of.

So, what's the right thing to do?

"The only thing necessary for the triumph of evil is for good men to do nothing."

Acknowledgment

I have had the good fortune of being blessed with a small circle of amazing girlfriends who reflect so much of who I want to be as a mother. Each one of you I take something from and have learnt a lot from.

Trecia. The months spent with you leading up to delivery have truly been some of the most valuable time in helping me mentally prepare for Liam's arrival.

To both my mom and dad, there are no words that will ever sufficiently express my appreciation and gratitude for the sacrifices that you have both made and how you continue to support me through all that life throws at me is more than I could ask for.

To my biggest supporter, my brother, Lance. God made no mistakes in bringing you and I together as siblings. I can't ever repay you. It's been a true learning experience watching you be such an involved father to my niece and nephew.

Dwayne, how fortunate are we? I look forward to this experience of watching our son grow, you trying to teach him the skills you have as a footballer, or how to treat a lady or any one of the million things I'm sure he will want only his dad to do with him.

To a remarkable young man that I have had the good fortune to manage, lead and learn from, Sammarko. Thank you for your support and excitement about my work. The irony in how it all unfolded doesn't escape me and you have been a blessing.

To the one that this is all for and in honor of, you are the greatest blessing of my life and this road, though short thus far, has not been easy but I would not trade it for anything. You have brought laughter to a part of my being that was sitting quietly but in great anticipation of you. I'm happy I waited as long as I did so I can give you an even better version of myself.

To my Creator, I am forever thankful and trust your process. Your grace and mercy are the only reason I am here.

About The Author

Marsha Flemmings built a career in the hospitality and travel industry that spanned eighteen years. Though halfway into that career she was the first to admit that it wasn't her passion, she and those around her couldn't deny her drive to help and serve others in pursuing their passion and attaining their goals. She led a record amount of her team to win top awards in the last half of her career and left a strong legacy in leadership.

Her conviction to continue to help lead and inspire others, especially young people led to her pursuit of becoming a Life Coach and launching her own company. An alum of Cornell University and University of Technology in Kingston, Jamaica she continues to equip herself to help others unlock their potential, move beyond limiting beliefs and design a legacy that transforms their lives and the lives of their families.

As is evidenced in her first book, Letters of Love and Legacy, she uses her journey, the successes and missteps, to help reinforce to anyone that they are able to design their legacy. Most recently she assumed her most important role, that of a mother and attributes much of her awakening to this experience.

Marsha Flemmings is available for coaching sessions and speaking engagements. To schedule a session visit www.marshaflemmings.com

Connect on social media

Facebook

www.facebook.com/marsha.flemmings

Instagram

www.instagram.com/marshaflemmings

LinkedIn

www.linkedin.com/in/marsha-flemmings

Made in the USA
Lexington, KY
16 March 2019